All the flowers have died

Sabrina Ellis

Copyright © 2018 Sabrina Ellis

All rights reserved.

All the flowers have died

Dearest Love

You were my beginning
The face I memorized
You found me
Better than I knew

Falling fast and soaring high
with love from every angle
I found you
Better than you knew

Kind and gentle spirit
Protector through the night

Two birds flying free

Taking flight to see new sights
 around life's treasured beauties

Overwatered

Sunflowers

Daisies

Orchids

Orange roses

You were the one I'd always have chosen

Winny

You and your southern drawl
Tall at 6'4"
Dark hair, brown eyes
like the desert mountains
you now called home
Swagger in your walk
with speed of determination
Gentle in your touch
like fear of rejection
Steady on the eyes
your gaze mesmerized
Heart as fragile as
a broken child
The love you give's not
handed out freely
To trust a soul is sacred
You're a being of mystique
and pure generosity
A man of the land
who wanders to and fro
You are who I call Winny

At Last

The look
My beanie
Talking heads
Congress
Rbar
Nightcap
4th floor
Saturday morning
Brand new day
Won my heart

Cousin's House

I was so sure, I made it soon
Outfit changes one Sunday afternoon

The nervous energy you held deep inside
Exploded through pictures, wear this or wear that?

My tension subsided because I knew
Everything I was feeling had to be true

A First Memory

We loved a good "bed time story"
That time I made you watch something scary
Flesh eating family
That was the night
the A/C was loud and
dogs barked in the morning
The light shown through
You in the kitchen
Blueberry pancakes and coffee
A happy Saturday
or Sunday, whichever days,
those were our days

Bisbee

It was like yesterday
Clean white linens
Shock Top on the porch

The way you looked at me
from across the table
spoke volumes to the future

Spicy Diablo proved to be
the food for romance

We danced to covers
Local bands seducing our ears

Those three little words
which turned into ten
ended the night on a high note

Creating a melody
We became a song of our own

Sweater Wearing Man

On any given day
That burnt orange sweater you wore
sunk onto your skin
like the mid afternoon sky

You and your high arched feet
Straight and narrow
My hands caressed hidden scars
from secrets you shared

The ink on your ribs
paints a meaningless story
Three natural marks on your chin
distinguish your beauty

Piano fingers
Rough exterior but soft to touch
Scruffy face on top of smooth cheekbones
Full head of hair curved to the right

Camouflaged rims perfectly placed
beyond the eyes that made me feel weak
A guiltless smile, endearing expression
Your sensitivity spills out true emotion

Voice of a southern man
Laughter so deep
Showed me your vulnerable side
Recognition of feeling real love

On any given day
That burnt orange sweater you wore
sunk onto your skin
like the mid afternoon sky

909 N 7th Ave.

Malbec
        Wine stained lips
Friday nights
        Thin crust pizza
Black truck
        Windows down
Music playing
        Ain't no sunshine

        Two stepping, Bobby Flay

        'Round the kitchen, Making dough

        Equipment missing, Cooking chicken

Shameless comfort
        Under your Mexican blanket
Nicholas Cage
        Dangling feet
Divisible by 5
        Dominoes on the high top
Acoustic guitar
        Our voices crashed in unison

Pajama Pants

Pink striped and rugged

I claimed them for a while

Talking heads
~~At~~ congress
R bar
~~after drinks~~ ?? nightcap
~~Apartment~~
walk home
~~wake up to you~~
~~thinking~~ of a new
4th floor
~~satu~~ friday nights, ~~thu cru~~

~~bri~~ Black truck, windows
~~dow~~ music played, Aint no s~~u~~
~~wo~~
chicken dish, cooking with
AGT on, stretched ac~~ross~~
~~shameless comfort,~~
~~soft snuggles,~~ under you~~r~~
walks downtown, Stargaz~~ing~~

OUR CITY.

~~long thing~~
~~stability~~
~~my e~~
~~work~~
~~let go~~

~~flowers~~
~~in full~~

~~time~~
wine stained li~~ps~~
~~thru crust pi~~
~~these week t~~
windows down
Ain't no Suns~~hine~~
~~these were th~~
dish, ~~w/ th~~
cooking ~~dinner like book~~
Agt on, stretch~~ed across~~
~~twin~~ Sof~~a~~
these were the ~~best days~~
you
~~face masks~~,
~~soft~~ snuggles, under the blanket

rhs
m/24
~5
~3-5
~30
~mahogany
~26

Creative
storyteller
Architect
Artist
Painter
Guitarist

Take two lives
watch them drown
~~words of~~ unspoken sto
accountable for nothi
the unraveling of a
~~true love story~~
Broken ~~down~~
down
tears
shed
Blood
pumps
love
released
circle
around

Ta
Wa
h
U

wemston

~~Two~~
It was like
clean sh
Shock to
the way
~~it~~, from
~~spicy~~ ~~spoke~~ volu
~~Hottest~~ ~~hottest~~ ~~to~~
~~Pool of bl~~
we danced ~~to~~
local bands
those three
which tur
ended the n
became
we c~~hatted~~
a song of

Grander than the ca

our love was grand
than the canyon
~~sweeter~~ larger than the sel
~~more delicious~~ than
grapes of Sonoita
More natural than
the state of Arkansas
~~just as~~ unique a
a bisbee ~~sto~~ ~~b~~
More lovely than th
dea A Sunset

Hands

Coffee press
Gripping handlebars
Manicured by a bite
Drivers seat
Hands entwined
You used to never let go

They were my favorite part
Masculine and strong, yet not a lot
of years behind them
They were a safe haven I'd not
experienced before

Strumming guitars
Cracking open bottles
Pen to paper
Watching you hold
your nephew for the first time
naturally your hands knew what to do

501

Country club and fancy things
Southern hospitality

Razorbacks and cheese dip
Golfing in the sunset

Purple cows
Riverwalk downtown

Nephews and nieces
Million dollar houses

Barbeque porch side
Blue VW rides

Wine and dine
Always family time

The Wall

5 women on the wall, dressed in white
Delicate beauties, each of their own
Marry who, what you know
My looks, resemblance of sisters
Surreal in my eyes
Fantasy I conjured in my head?
I owned white once, not my color
Too good to be true
 Means what it means
Not I
Not I
The 6th woman dressed in white
Hanging, delicate beauty
Not I

Thanksgiving After

Harry Potter could not save
Us
Arizona traveling backwards
Home
12 hours
12 long hours
Car ride spoke for itself that day
Turned to night
Hotel walls spoke louder than
Us two
6 more hours
Harry Potter tried again

Batch

Perfect Sundays
1 glass, we shared
Probably because we hadn't
much money or the level
of comfort we possessed
early on
Our idea of escaping for a little
Downtown walks to fill a void
or pleasure with
 one another
Key Lime doughnuts on our faces
Brainstorming new proposals
Art, work, moneymaking fantasies
The two of us were more alike
Did our mindset hinder our love?
Games we made up to pass the time
Saving birds at midnight
Never dull but
Sometimes quiet

Monterey

Signs I chose not to believe
A weekend away
Watching a movie in a theater
Not talking to one another
Monterey

Blue

You always looked best in blue
It's your favorite color
A symbol of you
Blue was the wine glass you drank from
The chambray shirt you wore
The jeans that fit your form just right
The feeling we were left with
The day we were over

Broken

Take two lives
Watch them drown
Words
Unspoken

The unraveling:
Tears shed
Blood pumps
Love released
Circle around

Desolate and Cold

Hold me
I reach out

Alone in the bed I lay
Why was I here?

7 months
to the day I last felt you

Footsteps crossed over footsteps
once walked upon before

I breathed the same air
Intoxicating rush

So near yet so far
Silent I remain

Slowly as I drive
my heart begins to heal

Our Love Was

Grander than the canyon

Larger than the Salt River

Groovier than the streets of Bisbee

Sweeter than the grapes of Sonoita

More natural than the state of Arkansas

Lovelier than the desert sunset

www.ingramcontent.com/pod-product-compliance
Lightning Source LLC
Chambersburg PA
CBHW041746040426
42444CB00004B/190